God bless you
Alphabet
&
Sightwords makeing sentence

Alphabet tracing

capital letter

A B C D E

F G H I J K

L M N O P

Q R S T U

V W X Y Z

ABCDEFGHIJKLMNOPURSTUDWXYZ

A

ABCDEFGHIJKLMNOPURSTUDWXYZ

B

ABCDEFGHIJKLMNOPURSTUDWXYZ

D

ABCDEFGHIJKLMNOPURSTUDWXYZ

E

ABCDEFGHIJKLMNOPURSTUDWXYZ

F

G

ABCDEFGHIJKLMNOPURSTUDWXYZ

H

ABCDEFGHIJKLMNOPURSTUDWXYZ

I

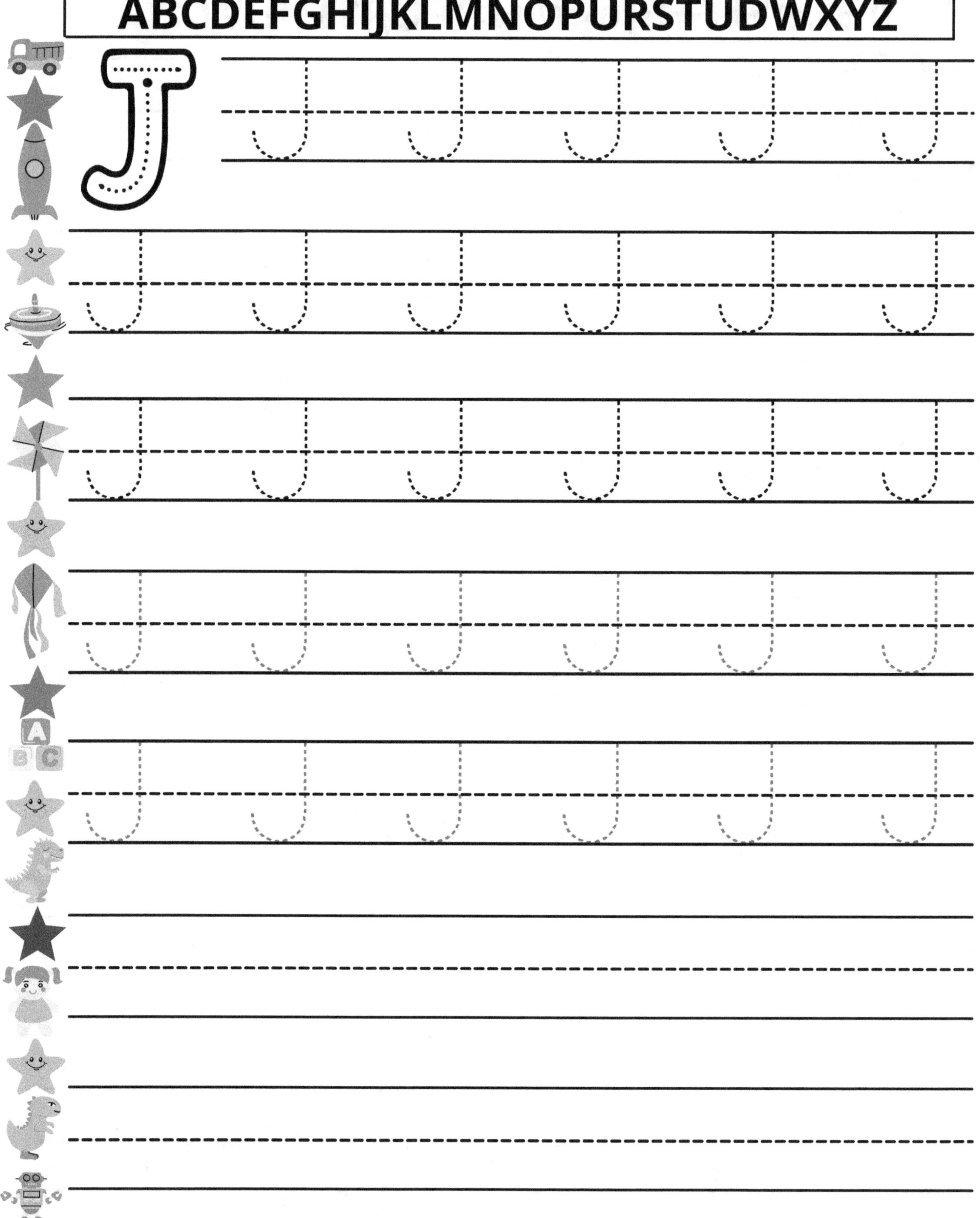

ABCDEFGHIJKLMNOPURSTUDWXYZ
J

ABCDEFGHIJKLMNOPURSTUDWXYZ

K

L

ABCDEFGHIJKLMNOPURSTUDWXYZ

M

ABCDEFGHIJKLMNOPURSTUDWXYZ

N

ABCDEFGHIJKLMNOPURSTUDWXYZ

ABCDEFGHIJKLMNOPURSTUDWXYZ

ABCDEFGHIJKLMNOPURSTUDWXYZ

Q

ABCDEFGHIJKLMNOPURSTUDWXYZ

ABCDEFGHIJKLMNOPURSTUDWXYZ

S

ABCDEFGHIJKLMNOPURSTUDWXYZ

T

ABCDEFGHIJKLMNOPURSTUDWXYZ

V

W

ABCDEFGHIJKLMNOPURSTUDWXYZ

ABCDEFGHIJKLMNOPURSTUDWXYZ

Y

Z

Alphabet tracing

small letter

a b c d e
f g h i j k
l m n o p
q r s t u v
w x y z

a

a b c d e f g h i j k l m n o p q r s t u v w x y z

a b c d e f g h i j k l m n o p q r s t u v w x y z

c   C   C   C   C   C

C   C   C   C   C   C

C   C   C   C   C   C

C   C   C   C   C   C

C   C   C   C   C   C

a b c d e f g h i j k l m n o p q r s t u v w x y z

a b c d e f g h i j k l m n o p q r s t u v w x y z

a b c d e f g h i j k l m n o p q r s t u v w x y z

g

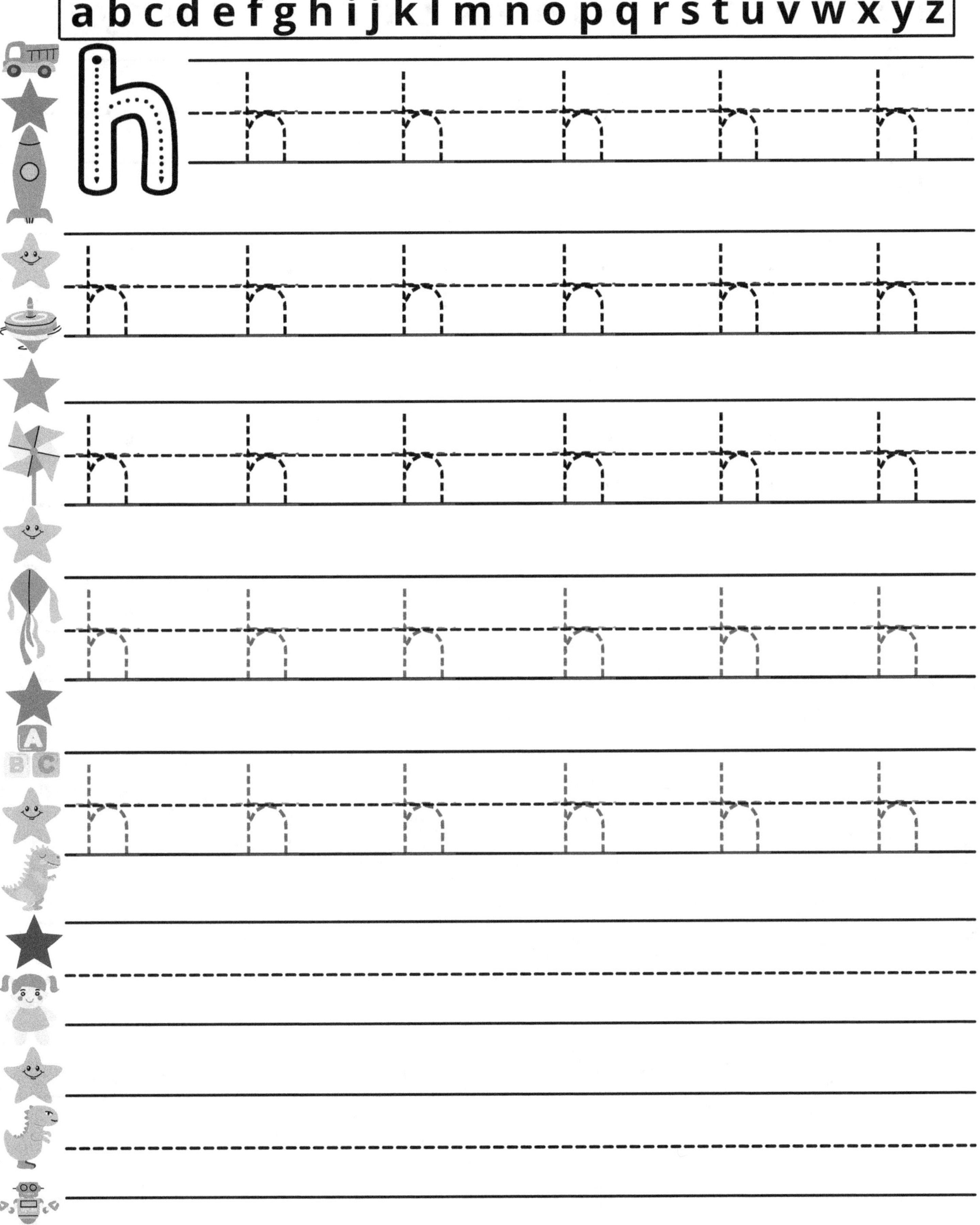

a b c d e f g h i j k l m n o p q r s t u v w x y z
h

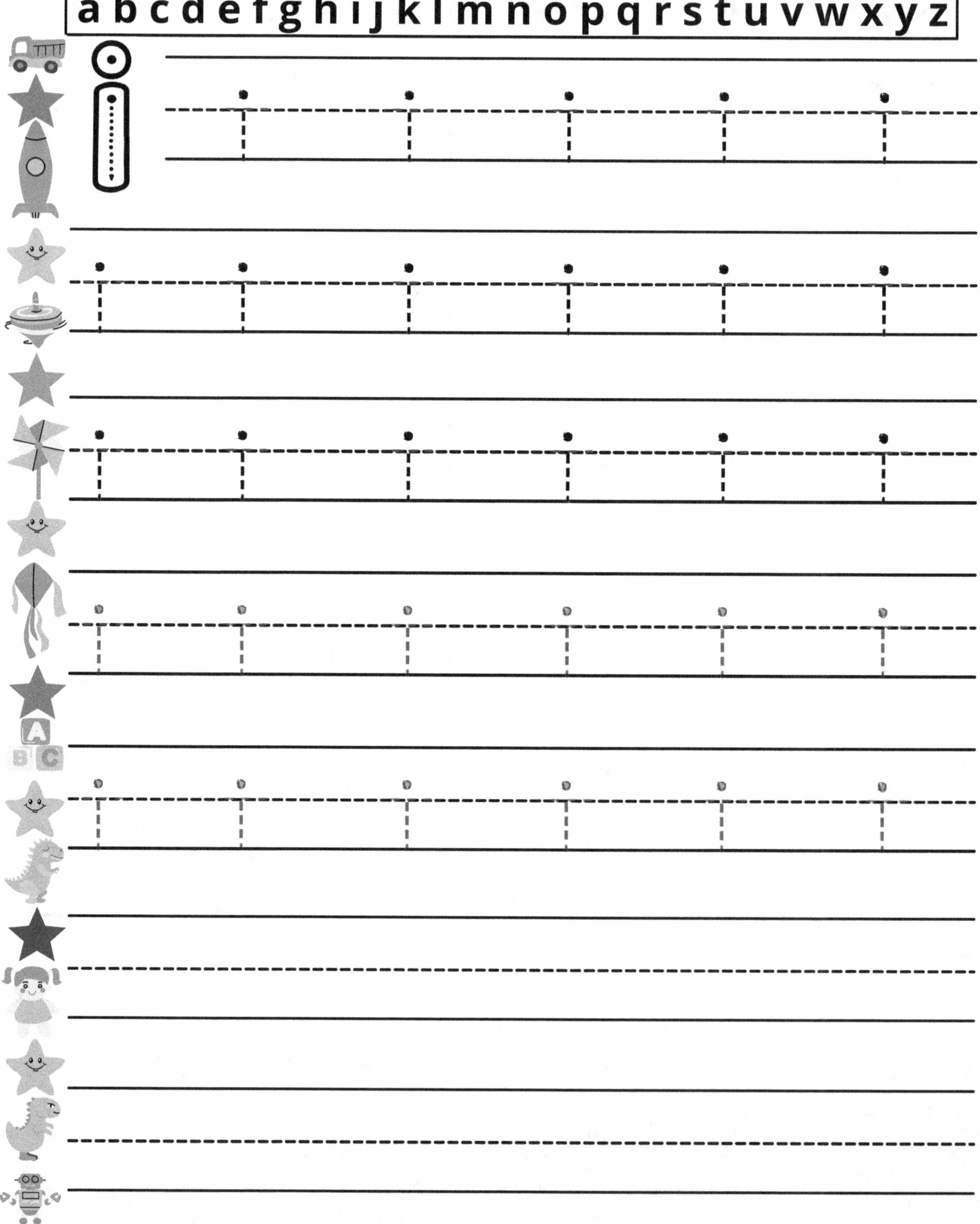

a b c d e f g h i j k l m n o p q r s t u v w x y z

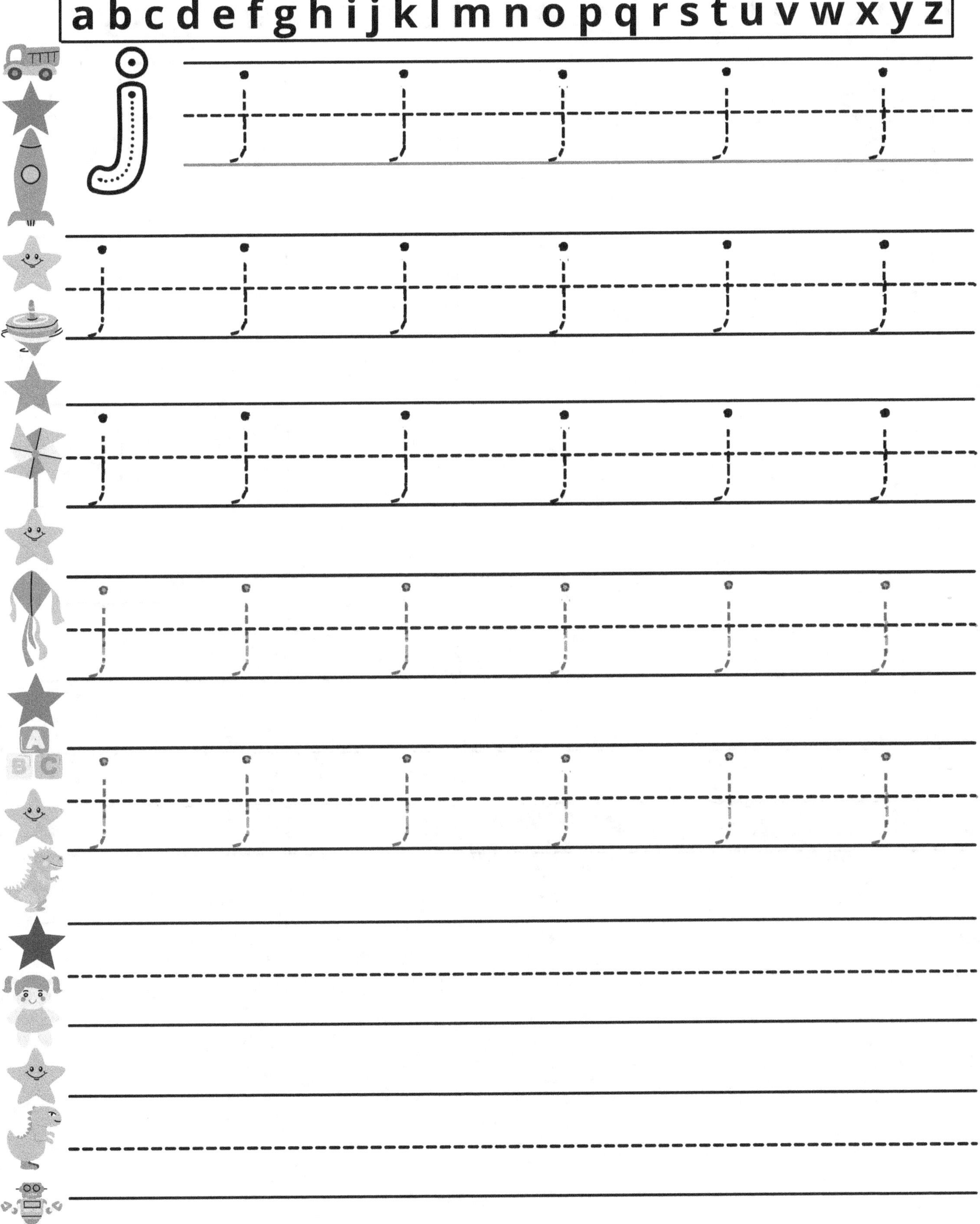

j

a b c d e f g h i j k l m n o p q r s t u v w x y z

k

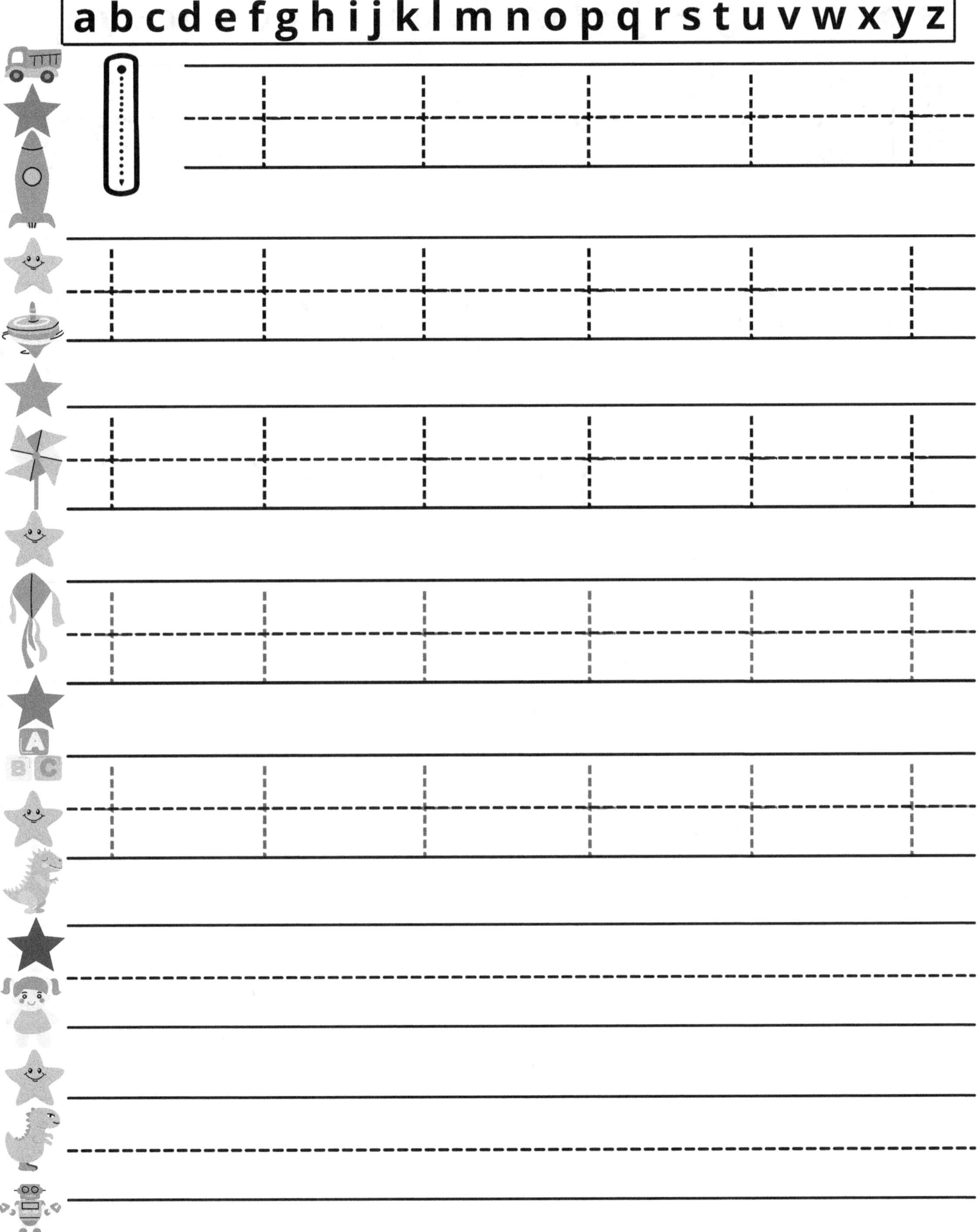
a b c d e f g h i j k l m n o p q r s t u v w x y z

m

n

a b c d e f g h i j k l m n o p q r s t u v w x y z

a b c d e f g h i j k l m n o p q r s t u v w x y z

a b c d e f g h i j k l m n o p q r s t u v w x y z

q

a b c d e f g h i j k l m n o p q r s t u v w x y z
r

s

a b c d e f g h i j k l m n o p q r s t u v w x y z

a b c d e f g h i j k l m n o p q r s t u v w x y z

W

X

a b c d e f g h i j k l m n o p q r s t u v w x y z

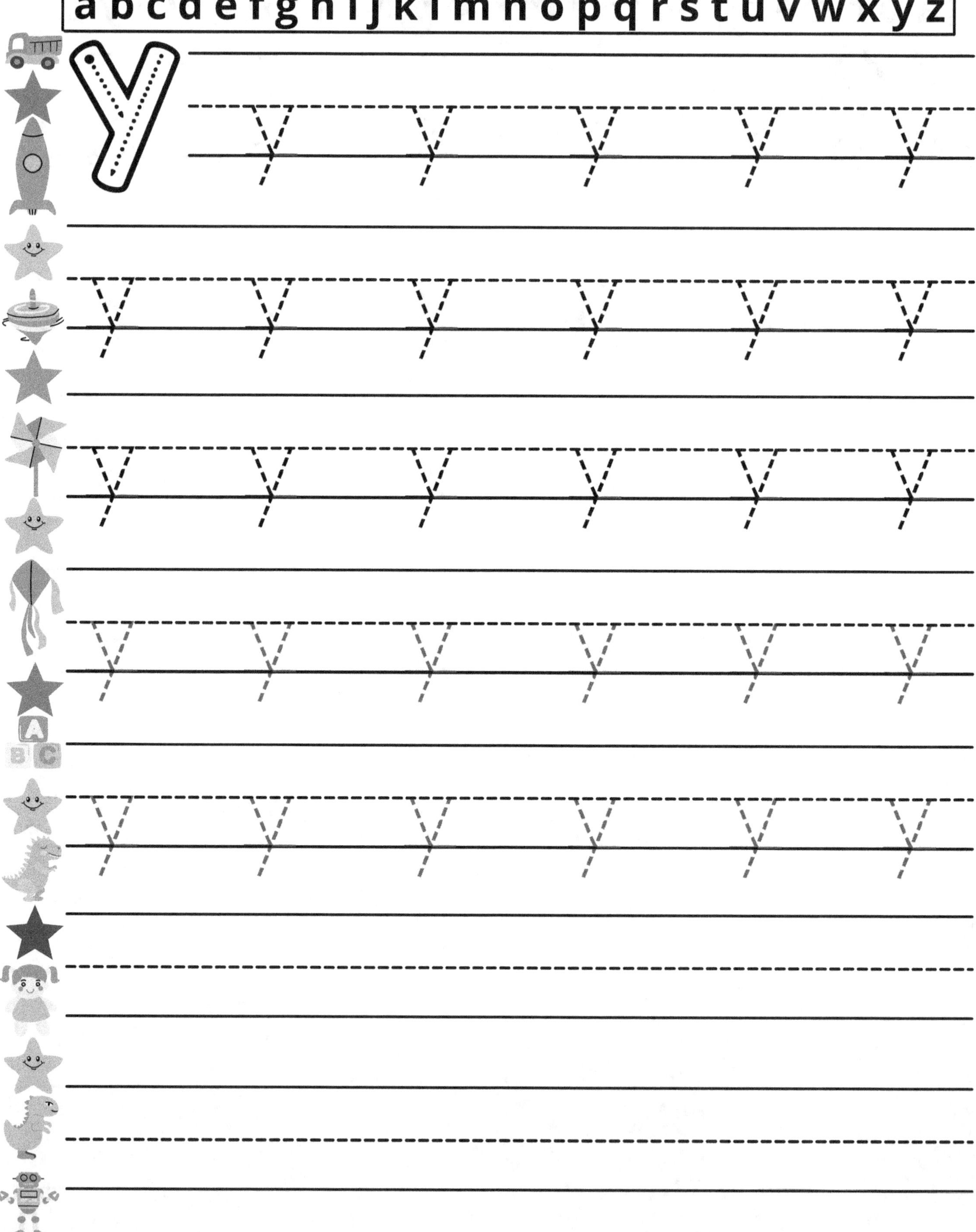

a b c d e f g h i j k l m n o p q r s t u v w x y z

Sightwords
makeing sentence

The gift is for _____ you.

Practice

the

the the the

Practice

____

pizza is hot.

The pizza is hot

Practice

of

Practice

Two ——— us jump.

Practice

and

and and and

Practice

I like cars ______ trucks.

I like cars and trucks

Practice

to

to   to   to

Practice

He walks ______ the store.

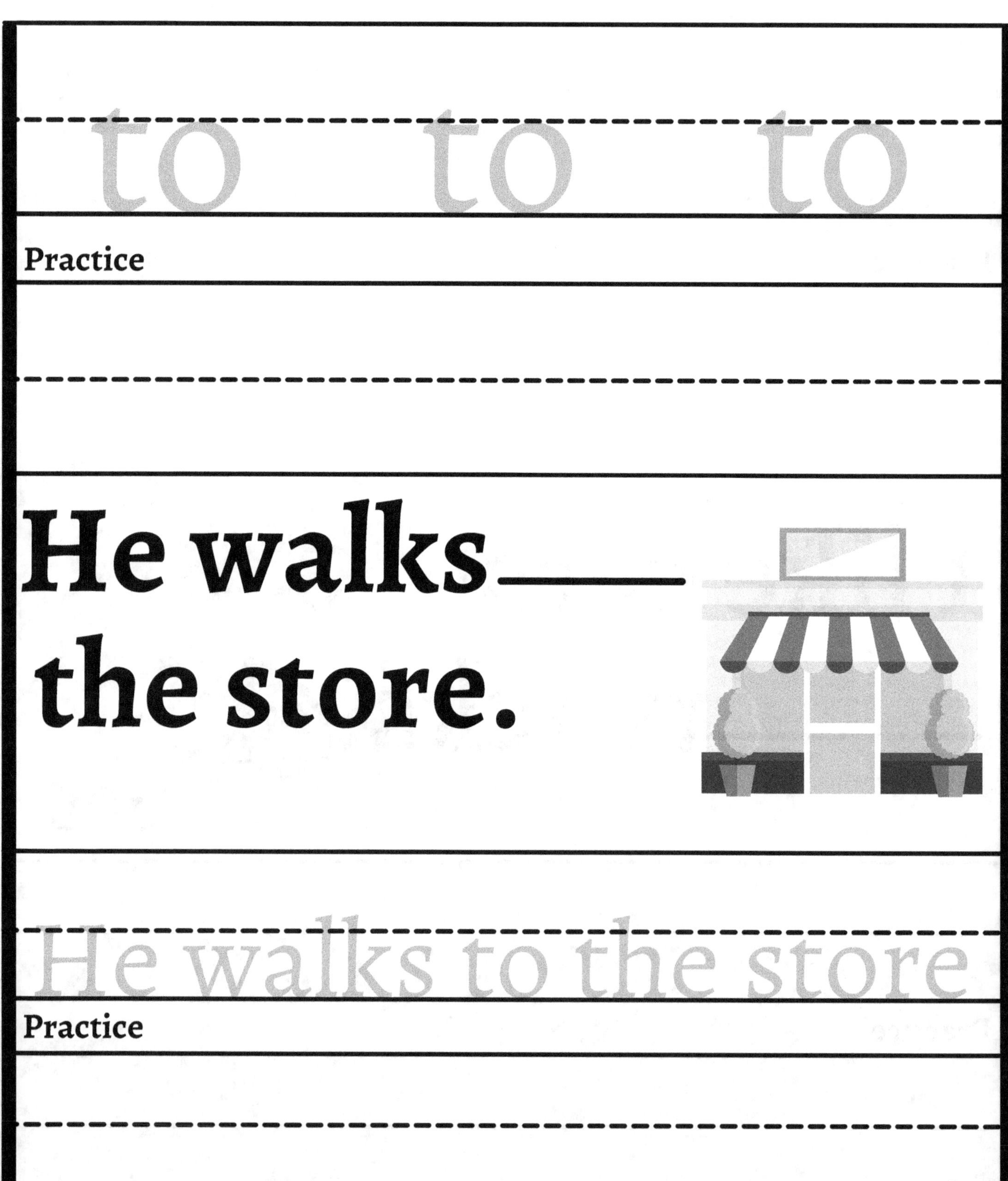

He walks to the store

Practice

a

a   a   a

Practice

I have — sweet cat.

I have a sweet cat

Practice

in

in in in

Practice

The food is _______ the bag.

The food is in the bag

Practice

is

is   is   is

Practice

The carrots ____ tasty.

The carrot is tasty

Practice

that

Practice

——— elephant is big.

Practice

it

it   it   it

Practice

______ is raining.

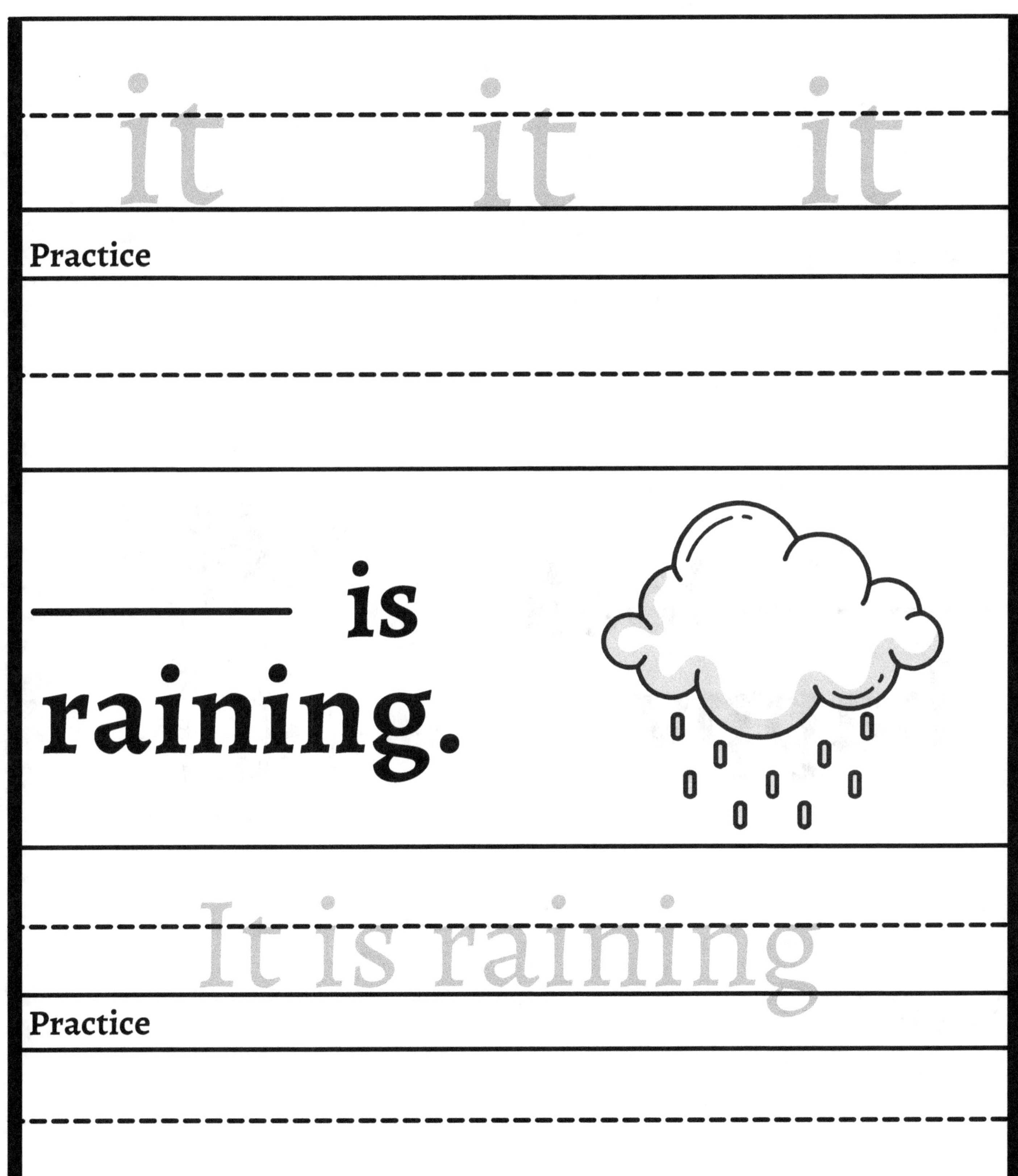

It is raining

Practice

you

Practice

_____ look happy.

Practice

he

he he he

Practice

_______ is eating.

He is eating

Practice

was

was was was

Practice

The light ——— bright.

The light was bright

Practice

for

for for for

Practice

The gift is _______ you.

The gift is for you

Practice

on

on   on   on

Practice

Drink is ____ the table.

Drink is on the table

Practice

are

are are are

Practice

You ——— a students.

You are a students

Practice

as

Practice

As soon_______ possible.

Practice

his his his

Practice

It is ____ ball.

It is his ball

Practice

with   with

Practice

My dog is
_____ me.

My dog is with me

Practice

they

they they

Practice

_________ **are tired.**

They are tired

Practice

i

i i i i i

Practice

—— am dancing.

I am dancing

Practice

at

at   at   at

Practice

We are _____ the market.

We are at the market

Practice

be

be be be

Practice

I will _______ at the library.

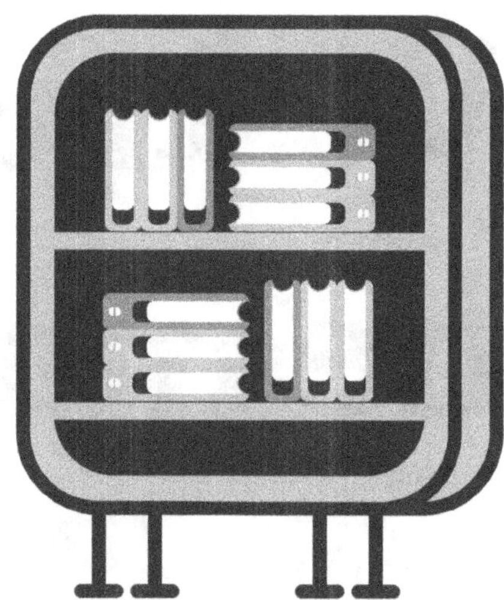

I will be at the library

Practice

this

this this this

Practice

_______ is my house.

This is my house

Practice

had

had had had

Practice

we _______ fun playing. 

we had fun playing

Practice

Practice

Where are you _____?

Practice

or

or   or   or

Practice

Give me apple ______ carrot.

Give me apple or carrot

Practice

have

Practice

I _________ two books.

Practice

but

but but but

Practice

I will go _______ tomorrow.

I will go but tomorrow

Practice

not

not not not

Practice

This is _______ my pen.

This is not my pen

Practice

by   by   by

Practice

The box is _______ the couch.

The box is by the couch

Practice

all

all all all

Practice

———— of us jump.

Practice

one

Practice

I have _______ toy car.

Practice

were

were were

Practice

We _____ camping yesterday.

We were camping yesterday

Practice

when

when when

Practice

__________ you
will go.

When you will go

Practice

she

she she she

Practice

__________ is my sister.

She is my sister

Practice

an

an   an   an

Practice

There is ______ cat at the zoo.

There is an cat at the zoo

Practice

there

there there

Practice

__________ are seven days in a week.

Practice

her

her her her

Practice

This is —— son.

Practice

their

their their

Practice

That is —————
tractor.

That is their tractor

Practice

can

can can can

Practice

I _______ do this job.

I can do this job

Practice

we

we we we

Practice

_____ like riding bikes.

we like ridiing bikes

Practice

about

about about

Practice

Tell me _____ yourself.

Tell me about yourself

Practice

up

Practice

Let's climb _______ that hill.

Practice

what what

Practice

_____ is your name.

Practice

out

out out out

Practice

we ran _____ of frozen food.

We ran out of frozen food

Practice

if

if   if   if

Practice

I will go _______ you are with me.

Practice

sad

sad sad sad

Practice

She ____ to wait by the tree.

Practice

some

some some

Practice

Let's buy ＿＿＿ fruit.

Let's buy some fruit

Practice

would

would would

Practice

I _______ like to dance.

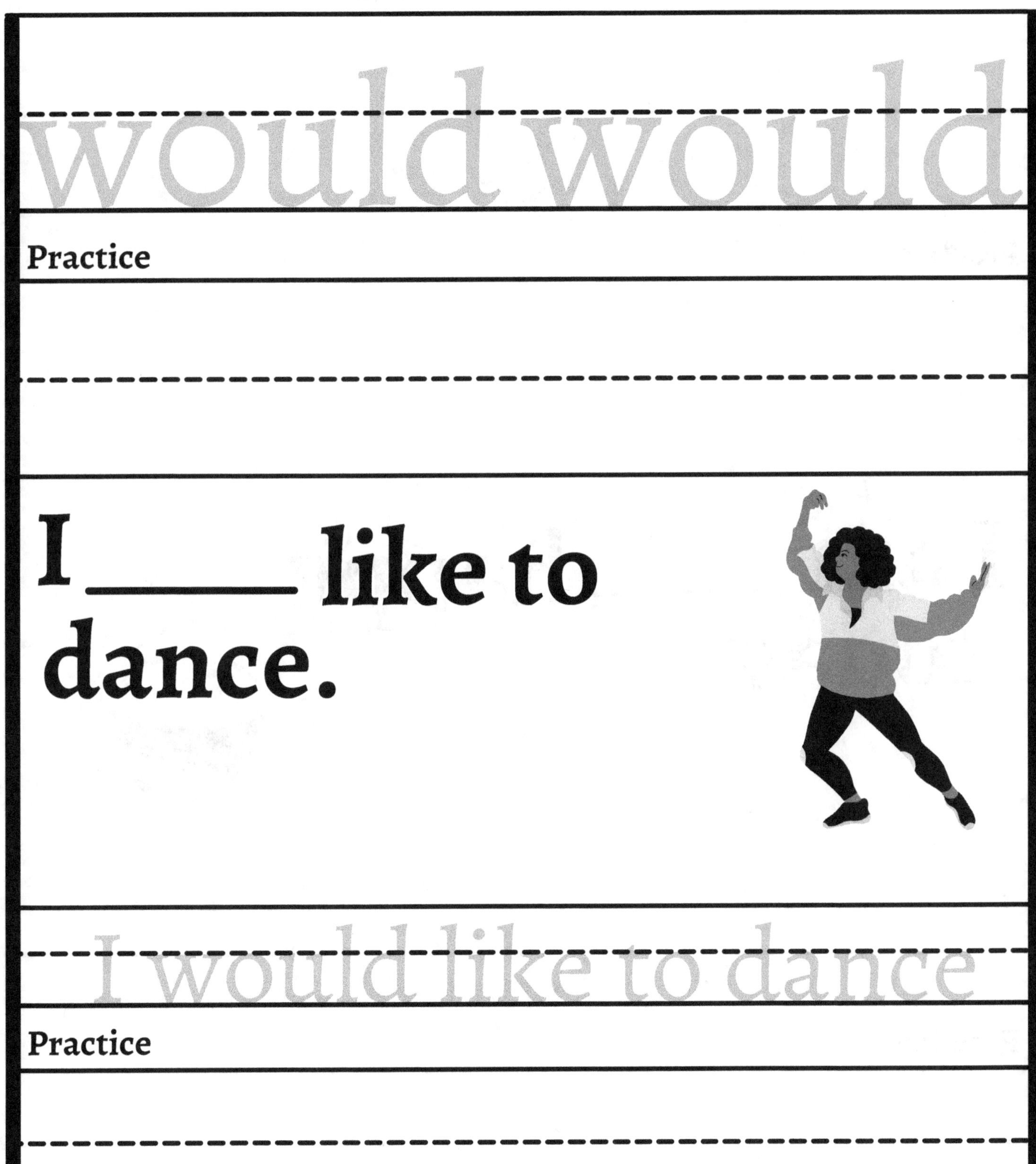

I would like to dance

Practice

SO

Practice

I am _______ happy today.

Practice

them

them them

Practice

When will i meet _____?

When will i meet them

Practice

people

Practice

Look at the

____

Practice

must

must must must

Practice

She _____ be feeling sick.

She must be feeling sick

Practice

more

Practice

we need _____ money.

Practice

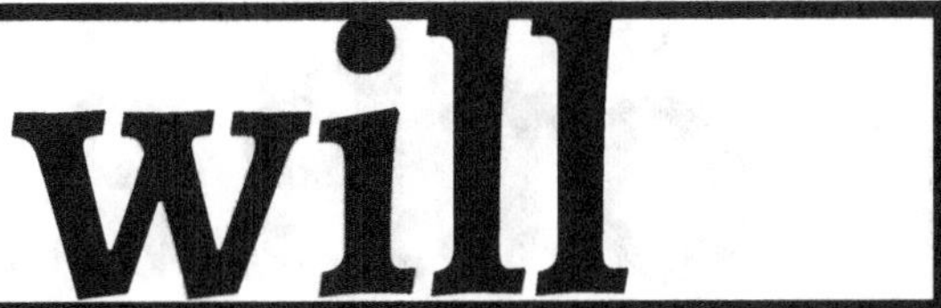

will

will will will

Practice

I _______ learn to sing.

Practice

other

Practice

Where is my ——— pen.

Practice

your

your your your

Practice

This is ______ book.

This is your book

Practice

into

into into into

Practice

I put the key
_______ the lock.

I put the key into the lock

Practice

which which

Practice

______ flag is taller ?

which flag is taller

Practice

do

do   do   do

Practice

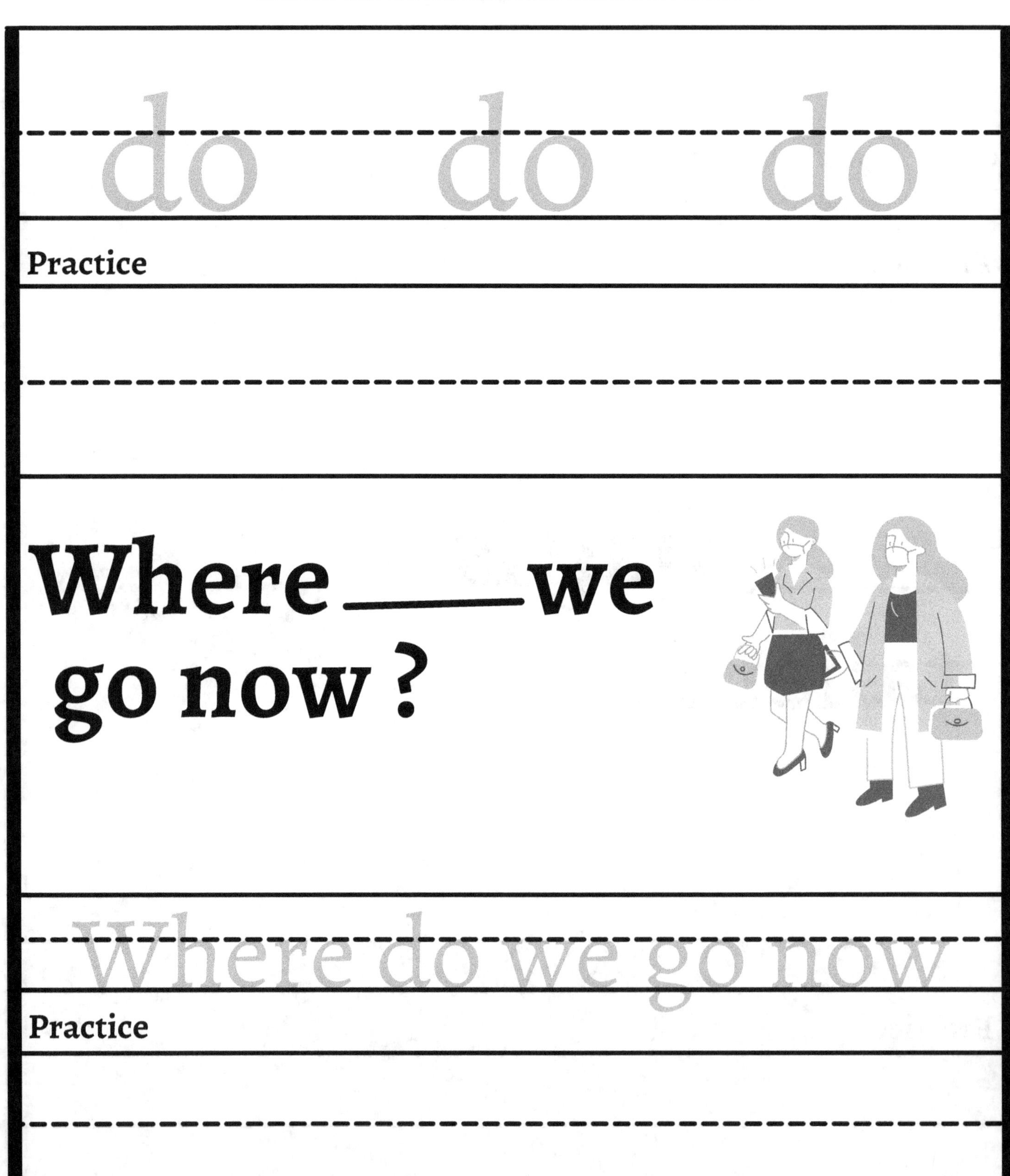

Where ____ we go now ?

Where do we go now

Practice

then

then then then

Practice

I liked to draw back _____

I liked to draw back then

Practice

no

no no no

Practice

_____ thankyou
i am full.

Practice

many

many many

Practice

I have _____ dog.

Practice

these

these these

Practice

_______ are my favorite pies.

These are my favorite pies

Practice

time

time time time

Practice

———— time
is it ?

What time is it

Practice

been

been been been

Practice

We have______ to canada.

We have been to canada

Practice

who

who who who

Practice

—— are you ?

Practice

has   has   has

Practice

He _____ a bike .

Practice

could

could could

Practice

I _______ eat the whole cake.

I could eat the whole cake

Practice

like

like like like

Practice

We _____ playing ball.

Practice

him

him him him

Practice

I will give ______ money.

I will give him money

Practice

then

then then then

Practice

Back _______
i took the bus. 

Back than i took the bus

Practice

how

how how how how

Practice

_______ **are**
you ?

How are you

Practice

may

Practice

She _____ get tired .

Practice

two

two two two

Practice

There are _____ triangles.

There are two triangles

Practice

only

only only only

Practice

There is _____ one banana.

There is only one banana

Practice

made

made made

Practice

I _____ a salad.

I made a salad

Practice

its

its *its* *its*

Practice

The dog ate _______ food.

The dog ate its food

Practice

Practice

He plays with car
_______ the time.

Practice

such

such such such

Practice

I have _______ a fun time.

I have such a fun time

**Practice

see

Practice

I _______ three blocks.

Practice

over over over

Practice

He walks _____ the bridge.

Practice

very

very very very

Practice

She is _______ happy.

She is very happy

Practice

first

first first first

Practice

This is her _______ car.

Practice

new

Practice

This is my
______ friend.

Practice

my

my my my

Practice

_____ family is awesome.

My family is awesome

Practice

also

---

also   also   also

Practice

I am ______
very cold.

I am also very cold

Practice

make

Practice

I can _____ art.

Practice

down

down down down

Practice

He walks _______ the stairs.

He walks down the stairs

Practice

now

now now now

Practice

She is reading right——

She is reading right now

Practice

way way way

Practice

I like the _____ you dance .

I like the way you dance

Practice

called

called called called

Practice

I _______ him with a cellphone.

I called him with a cellphone

Practice

did

did did did

Practice

I _______ my homework.

I did my homework

Practice

because

because because

Practice

I can not do it _______ its very hard.

I can not do it because its very hard

Practice

get

Practice

I can not _____ the door open .

Practice

through

through through

Practice

I can see ______ the camera lens .

I can see through the camera lens

Practice

after

Practice

_____ lunch i take a nap .

Practice

just just just

Practice

I _____ recived the package.

Practice

water

water water water

Practice

I drink ———— every day.

I drink water every day

Practice

where

where where

Practice

_______ is my luggage ?

Practice